Effective Hiring Strategies
Finding the Right Talent for Your Success

LMM Leadership Group
Business Performance & Leadership Specialists

LMM Leadership Group
Business Performance & Leadership Specialists

Contents

The Need to Do Better at Hiring

Your organization is only as good as the people that work for it.

This is the basis for just about everything as a manager. Our primary responsibility in managing is to get work done through other people. It is essential that managers recognize this, and instead of focusing only upon the 40 hours or more that they work a week, they instead need to take into consideration every hour of input that is available to them. This means that not only do managers need to consider their own hours, but also the hours of inputs provided by every employee that reports to the manager.

The ability to maximize performance of the total input hours that a manager has to get the work done that is assigned to him/her and the department depends largely upon the knowledge, skills, attitudes, and capabilities of those individuals working for the department or workgroup. This makes it essential to focus on the individual contribution of each and every employee as that is the basis upon which the manager's performance is evaluated. In other words, because the manager is evaluated upon the total productivity and effectiveness of the group over which he or she supervises, the manager's performance is directly linked to the collective performance of all individual employees.

If an organization wants to improve its performance, and an organization's performance is really only as good as the collective performance of its employees, then there are really only two ways to improve organizational performance: (a) develop and improve performance among current employees or (b) import new talent that performs a higher level.

The focus of this discussion is on the second option - importing - or the hiring process which involves bringing new people into the organization. If you want the best performance from your organization, you need the best performance from your people, which means that you need to bring in the best talent that is available to you. While you may have been lucky in the past and found some good talent, rarely does it happen by itself. It is important to understand a few processes that could help you to improve your chances of bringing in quality talent through your hiring process.

Before You Begin to Hire

The Most Common Question

Understanding that your goal is to find the best talent available and bring them into your organization, it is unfortunate that one of the most common questions that the Human Resources Department receives prior to a hiring process is:

Do you have a copy of the questions that we used last time?

Many, including Albert Einstein, have been credited with the definition of insanity – continuing to do what you have always done and expecting something different. If you did not have the right talent before, then why use the same processes to find your next hire?

Consider Your Past Experiences

An evaluation of past experiences (positive and negative) can help to improve future processes and your success.

Consider Your Challenges

Before hiring a new person, take some time to consider past experiences.

- What are your most common complaints about the hiring process?
- What are you most common complaints about new employees you have hired in the past?
- What do you wish you could do to improve the hiring process for your positions?

By taking a few moments to reflect upon the challenges of the past, you may be able to take a step back and consider how to avoid them or fix them for your next process. Without considering some of the hiccups from the past, you may continue to perpetuate them as you move forward.

Some will blame Human Resources, managers, employment laws, or other things from being able to allow them to overcome these challenges. Chances are good that by taking this first step, you may be able to achieve the goals that you want to by making some minor adjustments.

Consider Your Successes

Similarly, managers should also take the time to consider what has worked well in the past. Chances are good that over time you have developed some techniques or strategies that have actually produced quality results. Take some time to consider what has worked well in the past, what the results have been from using those processes, and consider if there are ways to improve that strategy.

What Are You Looking For?

Before beginning to write down your first interview question, or submitting your advertisement to post, you need to understand what you are looking for.

Unless you have a clear, vivid image of what you are looking for in your next candidate, it will be challenging to bring in the top talent that you need. In other words, *if you don't know what you're looking for, how will you know when you get it?*

There are some key sources of information that we will discuss in the next section that can help you collect the information that will help define the position as you need it to be filled. At the same time, you probably have some key performance indicators that you want to have accomplished from the new person coming into the position.

Top Performer Profile

Before you begin the process, you will want to start to generally define "what does good look like?" This goes beyond the simple information that is contained in the job description. While that may be a valuable source to collect some ideas, there are other factors that you must take into consideration. Below is a list of questions that you may consider asking yourself to begin to identify what exactly you are looking for in the new talent.

- What did the previous incumbent do that MUST be performed by the replacement?
- What did the previous incumbent NOT DO that MUST be performed by the replacement?
- What level of skill should you be looking for in the replacement?
- What level of expertise should be the aspiring for the new candidate within the scope of the job classification?
- What type of personality would best fit within this position given the job, coworkers, the culture of the department, and organizational culture?
- How can we recognize those personality traits?
- What additional competencies must this person have to be successful in this position? (e.g., leadership, good communication skills, conflict resolution, multitasking skills, ability to work under pressure, great interpersonal relationship skills, etc. depending upon the job)
- What additional capacities must this person have to be successful in this position? (e.g., ability to learn quickly, ability to adapt, ability to critically think, ability to problem solve, etc. depending upon the job)

During this first step, you will not get it right the first time. This is only a starting list to help you get started. This will provide you some essential guidance so you can have a greater understanding of what you're looking for. You will continue to refine this during the next few stages.

Preparing to Hire the Right Talent

Now that you have created an essential outline of the "Top Performer Profile", let's consider some other areas to review in preparation for hiring. (Keep in mind that we have not yet advertised for the position. That will come later.)

Job Description

A key document to help you define the position is the job description. In most cases, Human Resources maintains current job descriptions. As you are looking to hire a new person for this position, this is an excellent time to review the entire job description to ensure its accuracy. If it is not accurate, this is the time to fix it and communicate with Human Resources to ensure accuracy of the job description. The job description typically includes the essential and other functions of the job, core requirements, qualifications, scope of the position, physical requirements of the job, and other factors that are important to the successful performance of the incumbent in the position.

Other Position Information

In some cases, there may be information related to a given position such as policies, procedures, or instructions that are relevant. For example, an employee who works on a production line may have specific requirements that they must fulfill as part of their position that may not necessarily be included in the job description. Considering specific requirements based upon the position, responsibilities, and impact to other employees within the department (such as those "down the line" in a manufacturing environment) can help to improve accuracy of expectations.

Department Information

There may be specific policies, procedures, guidelines, and cultural elements that are specific to your department that will be essential to consider when hiring a new person. It is not just the job that you are hiring for, but also a new team member for your department. Consider the mechanics of your team and what "good fit" looks like and how you can define it, describe it, and identify it. This may also include information pertaining to specific initiatives and priorities that you currently have in the department and for which your new hire could assist in accomplishing.

Organizational Goals and Objectives

Every position should be aligned to the goals and objectives of the organization. Consider how this position contributes to department goals and objectives as well as organizational goals and objectives. Review the organization's strategic plan, core competencies, key values, and other consistent requirements applicable to all employees. Include some of these elements into your list.

List of Personal Characteristics and Competencies

Consider once again what would be required or ideal for a candidate to have or be in order to be successful in the position. This may include those qualities that are absolutely required, are nice if they have, or are bonuses if they bring in such characteristics and competencies.

Advertising for the Position

Now that you have spent considerable time defining the position and what you need from the new incumbent, it is time to prepare for the advertising process.

The reason that the initial steps are recommended is to clearly understand what you want and why you want it from this position. This will help to improve the focus and strategy as you advertise for the position.

Advertising and recruiting follows many of the same principles as marketing. Of importance is the concept of "niche marketing" or "target marketing". This is simply understanding what your product is, what it can do, who is the most likely candidate to want this product (including demographics), where they are located, and how to get the message to them in a way that will entice them to make a purchase.

Similarly, in advertising for a position, we need to understand the following:

(1) What is the position and what we need from it
(2) How it fits in the organization and why it is important
(3) What is the common profile of an individual who would best perform in this position
(4) Where is the ideal candidate currently living, working, performing
(5) How to craft and deliver a message that will reach the ideal candidate

In many organizations, the standard approach is to advertise in the local newspaper. This is still a viable approach to sending information out to the general public. However, the effectiveness of this approach by itself is typically less effective.

Keep this in mind: WHERE is your best future candidate currently?

The answer is probably: Working for your competition.

By advertising in the local paper and only taking that approach, the individuals who you want the most are probably not looking in the want ads of the local newspaper. This means that you need to find other ways to reach out to them and communicate the opportunity to them.

Additionally, if your future employee is currently working elsewhere, chances are good that they would need an enticing reason to leave their current employment to come to you.

For many, this approach is significantly different than the current approach that they may take. In many organizations, the manager simply sends a request to Human Resources to conduct the recruitment and hiring processes. Even if that is the case, there are several things that the manager can do to improve the ability to identify, find, and attract the best talent beyond that which Human Resources currently does.

Recruitment Strategies for Managers

The nature of your employees, both current and future, has changed significantly even over the past decade. The approaches that were used in the past to identify and attract candidates may no longer be the most effective approach. Below are some strategies that you may consider in order to reach out to your applicant pool as you have defined in the previous steps. This is by no means a comprehensive list of options for you. They are just a handful of considerations that may be effective for you to try.

Traditional Advertising

The previous section discussed the lower effectiveness in only using traditional print advertising. This does not mean that traditional advertising does not work. It just means that when used by itself, it is not necessarily the most effective approach to finding the best talent. You can use traditional advertising, but be sure that you craft the message in a way that is attractive to candidates. Regurgitating the language from the job description is not very attractive. Give your potential future hires a reason to read the advertisement. Better yet, entice them through your advertising to want to come to work for you.

Targeted Advertising

In the case of professional level employees, there are trade magazines, publications, websites, and other sources of information that are specific to particular professionals. Spending a few extra dollars to advertise in a professional journal or publication makes sense if you are trying to reach the highest number of qualified candidates who may not otherwise be actively searching for a new position.

Social Media

Social media sources are ABSOLUTELY key to your success in reaching out and connecting with qualified individuals. If you are not yet involved in social media, now is the time to begin. There are some basic strategies that you can utilize as well is perhaps more advanced approaches. Let's consider some of the more essential approaches that could help you to reach out to applicants. We are going to begin with "The Big 4".

- Facebook: If Facebook were a country, it would be the second-largest country in the world by population (second only to China). Nearly everybody has a Facebook account. By establishing your own Facebook site, integrating it into your company, and then promoting through the channels that are available through Facebook advertising, you may be able to reach many, many individuals who may not otherwise hear that you are hiring. The advertising available through Facebook allows you to define your demographics, geography, and even the budget that you're willing to spend to send out the message that you're hiring. The cost is typically significantly cheaper than any print advertising that you do.

- Twitter: Twitter is an online form of text messaging to the world. If you have established your personal account or if the organization has one, consider building a followership of users by reaching out and connecting with as many people as you can who are pertinent to your industry, interest, etc. As you continue to interact on Twitter and build your following, as you send out your short messages this will continue to reach additional folks. It's not just a matter of "help wanted", but incorporating a message in with other messages that are of interest to other users.

- LinkedIn: LinkedIn is a professional networking site. At the professional level, most individuals have a LinkedIn account. By creating an attractive LinkedIn account for yourself, and then reaching out to others with similar interests in your industry or specific individuals, you can build a following. Within LinkedIn you have the ability to search for other people based upon demographics and geography which can help you to target those to whom you send an invitation to follow. A subscription is also available that gives you premium access to send messages to individuals. This means that as you find an individual who would qualify for the position, you could use LinkedIn to directly connect with them and tell them about the position and why you are interested in them.

- YouTube: The final social media site for this discussion is YouTube. For those who still consider it to be a repository of silly videos, it's time to go check out the current YouTube model. YouTube is the second-largest search engine in the world (second only to Google, who owns YouTube). Sending your message is important, and as they say, "A picture is worth 1000 words". If a picture is worth 1000 words, a short video is worth much more. Creating a fun and attractive video that showcases your company can help candidates to visualize what it would be like to work in your organization. As you build a fun and short YouTube video, not only will it be posted on the YouTube site, but you can blend that video into the other social media sites as well. Again, this adds the visual component to the advertisement.

Networks

As a manager, chances are good that you know people within the industry. You have colleagues who work for other organizations and may be exactly who you are looking for, or you have friends and connections throughout the industry, country, or world with similar interests. By continuing to build your own personal network, and then reaching out to them when you have a position that is available, this can bring you some of the best qualified applicants. Connect with them and mention, "Hey, John, I have this position that's available and I am looking for qualified candidates. While you are doing great in your current job I was wondering if you had anyone in mind that might be a good candidate or who might be interested in it." This kind of approach takes the pressure off of avoiding the appearance of pirating individuals. If the direct contact is interested, they would let you know right away. At the same time, it expands your "word-of-mouth" approach to getting the message out there.

Associations and Memberships

Most professionals belong to one or more professional associations as an active member. You may tap into your personal membership and spread the message about the available positions. Similarly, depending upon the position that is open for which you are recruiting, you may consider which professional associations would most likely be connected to that position. You can then reach out to that association and identify methods to get the message out such as advertising on their webpage, printouts of their publications, or other approaches.

Direct Targeting

Another approach may be to simply identify through research and homework who is doing this type of position in other companies. You may then reach out with a phone call, invitation to lunch, or letter to let them know of the opportunity. While this may be considered by some to be a form of "poaching", is one of the most common practices out of the market today. While you may not prefer this kind of approach, consider this: your competition is probably doing it to your employees right now.

Establishing Evaluation Criteria

As you have established a list of needs and a top profile for potentially the best candidates, it is now time to establish the evaluation criteria to be used in the interview process. In other words, you are going to define how you will know what "good" looks like from your candidates.

At this point you have established your list of wants and needs for your candidates. It is now time to break those into three distinct groups:

- **Deal Breakers**: These are the things that are going to be an automatic "no go" for the candidates. This may be based upon their responses, their background, their experiences, education, appearance (e.g., professional), demeanor, or other key indicators. In other words, the deal breakers are those elements that no matter what, you cannot possibly live with the person who brings it with them to the job.

  Too many managers tend to weigh out the pros and cons of the candidates and allow them to come on board with the sense that the pros will outweigh the cons. This may be the case in some situations; however, these deal breakers are things that no matter what other qualities or redeeming factors that the candidate has, these are things that by themselves disqualify an individual.

  For example, when hiring administrative support staff, you may find an individual to be very pleasant, communicate well, have a great demeanor and appearance, and otherwise appear to be a well-qualified candidate. Through a sit-down interview process, the individual may give you the best answers, be very refined in the responses, and otherwise appear to be the best candidate for the position. If, however, this administrative support candidate is not proficient in Word, Excel, or e-mail, then no matter how nice the person is, they will not be effective in the support function. In this case, the proficient use of business software is a deal breaker if they did not have that level of proficiency that you require.

- **Core Requirements**: These are simply establishing those requirements that a candidate must have to be qualified for the position. Keep in mind that not every candidate who could be qualified may have a high level of proficiency in all required areas. For this reason, it is essential that you establish thresholds for each of the core requirements. For example, some core requirements may require 100% proficiency. In others, however, while it would be nice to have 100% proficiency, you could live with, say, 80% proficiency for them to be effective in the job. As you establish these thresholds, you will also want to identify how to recognize what those levels of proficiencies are and how to measure them.

- **"Plus 1" Qualifications**: This final category includes those qualifications that the candidate has that are nice to have, but are not necessarily required for the position. If the candidate comes in to an interview process and meets the core requirements of the position, and does not possess any of the deal breakers that would otherwise disqualify him or her, then if they have an additional skill, experience, quality, or qualification, that may be identified as such a nice to have quality that made help in setting them apart from the other candidates.

Creating Your Interview Script

In the previous sections you identified what you're looking for in the position and the criteria by which to measure and evaluate a candidate's qualification level in those requirements. It is now time to establish your script. This does not necessarily mean something that you will read to every candidate nor does it only include the list of questions that you will use through the process. It is more like a "map" to guide you through the conversation with the candidate.

What Do You Want to Find Out?

Your first step in creating your interview script is to establish what you want to find out from the individual. As you review the requirements of the position, consider this question: What should I or can I ask that will help me to know if they meet this requirement?

In cases where a simple verbal response is not adequate to demonstrate proficiency in the requirements, you may ask a similar question: How can I determine if this applicant has the level of skill or qualification that I need?

As you can imagine, some of the responses to these self-imposed questions may result in questions to be asked directly of the candidate in a sit-down interview process. Others, however, cannot simply be discovered through conversation. You may need to consider other methods by which you can establish if they have the level of proficiency in the skills that you require. In other words, what is the best way to find out if they have a certain level of proficiency within one of the requirements? We will discuss this later on.

How Will You Determine What You Are Looking For?

Creating a list of what you want to find out and perhaps some methods that may help you to obtain this information is a starting point. In some cases it will require a sit-down face-to-face interview while others would require a more nontraditional or hands-on approach to demonstrating skill or competency.

As you establish how to discover the information, you also need to establish measures to consistently determine the level to which the candidate is meeting the requirements. In other words, you will want to establish clear measures as to how a person meets a certain requirements and to what level he/she might meet those requirements.

In the case of a sit down interview process, you will begin to create a list of questions that will help guide you and any other interviewers to determine if the candidate has the knowledge, skills, attitudes, and capabilities to be able to perform well the position. Once you list out the questions for your interview, you will want to establish examples of what you are looking for from the candidates. You may identify what answers would disqualify the candidate completely, what answers would meet the expectations or otherwise satisfactorily demonstrate that the candidate is qualified, and then those answers that would indicate that they are not only qualified, but maybe exceptionally qualified for the position.

By both listing the questions and then identifying the desired responses or at least examples of what "good" looks like in response, this helps you to maintain consistency in the evaluation of your candidates. As you bring others into the process, they will be using the same criteria as well, which improves consistency among interviewers and assessors in your process.

Other Interview Preparations

There are several details involved in the organization, preparation, and execution of the interviews. While you may have an administrative support person to assist you with the details, it is important for you to be aware of some of the logistics involved in organizing the selection process. Some of these considerations include the following:

The Interview Committee

If you use multiple parties or individuals in the selection process, you'll need to consider a few things.

- Who SHOULD be on the committee – It is important to identify the most effective individuals to participate in the selection process. Those who are connected to the position more closely or have a good understanding as to what the desired requirements are and how to assess it are typically best. You will also want to consider the politics behind the position in case there are individuals that ought to be part of the process for internal purposes.

- Who SHOULD NOT be on the committee - Be selective in the consideration of individuals to participate in the process. To include somebody in the process just for the sake of including them, and where those individuals would not be able to actively contribute to the determination of a candidate's qualifications, is typically a disservice to both them and you. Also consider those individuals who have not participated well in previous selection processes and consider whether or not it is appropriate to include them in the process.

- Role – selection vs. recommendation - One of the greatest internal challenges that exist is when a committee is used in the selection process, but their role is not clearly defined. When the committee is utilized, and names are submitted by the committee to a final decision-maker, feelings tend to get hurt when the decision-maker does not take into consideration the prioritization by the committee or they otherwise make a final decision that is contrary to the efforts of the committee. If you use a committee as a way to conduct an initial screening process, make sure that they are aware of their role. If, however, their role is to narrow down and identify the finalists of the process in rank order, you must respect that in your final decision-making.

- Training committee members - It is essential that individuals involved in the selection process are adequately trained to do so. This improves both the effectiveness in their ability to serve as a selector and also substantially reduces the potential liability that could exist should that interviewer say or do the wrong thing. This helps to create greater consistency across your organization regarding the processes and procedures related to interviewing.

Physical Location Preparations

There are several physical preparations that are needed to ensure a smooth process for both you and the candidate.

- Room location - Be sure to reserve the room location for your interviews prior to the interview taking place. Having a candidate show up and then looking for a room gives a bad impression, especially when you end up in a less than ideal location. Find a location that is quiet, private, and comfortable for both you and the candidate.

- Room set-up - How you set up the room for the interview speaks volumes. For example, a large room with a large table, where an interview panel sits on one side of the table and the candidate on the other side creates a significant feeling of distance and formality. A few chairs around a small table can allow for closer interaction and greater personal connection with the candidate. Setting up a room with chairs and without a table or desk between the interviewers and the candidate creates a very open environment. It may take some individuals some time to become comfortable in a setting such as this is there is not any table to hide behind for greater security. At the same time, there is greater openness and ability to connect with the other person with this arrangement.

- Creating a sound first impression - The interview process is not only the time for you to select the candidates, but it is also a time for your potential talent to interview and evaluate you. The physical location preparations can go a long ways to clearly demonstrate professionalism and organization.

- Supplies in the room - Also be sure to supply the room with adequate materials for the interview process. Ensure that there is water for the candidate and the interviewers, paper, pens, and other materials as would be necessary by either party.

Materials Preparation

Another consideration that will help to ensure smoothness to the process is to ensure that sufficient materials are made available through the interview process. Examples of materials that are common that should be made available to all parties include:

- Copies of resume, application materials for selection committee members

- Agendas for all members which includes a list of all of those candidates to be interviewed, time schedule, and other pertinent information

- Interview questions or guidelines to follow to ensure consistency throughout the interview process

- Evaluation forms so each interviewer has a form for each candidate upon which to make comments or otherwise evaluate candidate

- Other information and materials necessary to ensure a smooth selection process.

Selection Tools

Many managers consider the primary selection tool to be the sit-down, face-to-face interview. This approach can be an effective way to refine the selection of candidates as it provides a method to get to know the applicant more personally. When assessing considerations such as "fit", the personal interview can be an effective method. However, it is not designed to be a one-size-fits-all approach to selecting the best candidates.

Several tools exist for managers. Not all selection tools will work for all situations. However, the following provides an overview of tools that are available to managers to consider incorporating into their selection processes to improve the ability to evaluate the level of proficiency held by individuals.

Resume Review

A common approach to evaluating candidates is to review the resume. While this is typically the first step, it is also strongly recommended that it be done according to the priorities set as you prepared your Top Performer Profile. By having prepared your Profile far in advance, and by identifying your "deal breakers" in advance, your first review of resumes should go faster and more efficiently. You will be able to screen out the individuals who are not qualified for more quickly because you have prepared your list of what you're looking for.

Supplemental Questionnaires

A considerable amount of time is spent during the sit-down interview asking questions that may be important to know, but may not be the best use of time given the limited schedule that you have to talk with a candidate. There may be some questions that can be asked and effectively answered outside of the face-to-face interview. Many managers have found the use of a supplemental questionnaire to be an effective second step to identifying quality candidates. Following the resume review, hiring managers may send out a supplemental questionnaire with a handful of questions that can help the manager to identify qualified applicants. Depending upon the questions that are asked in the supplemental questionnaire, you may be able to evaluate the candidate's ability to process information, write professionally, present in a way that appears professional, assess their critical thinking skills as they answer the questions, and demonstrate other skills that may come as you review the responses. In some situations, the candidate actually does not respond to the questionnaire, which may be a clear indication that he/she just wasn't that interested in the job. The use of supplemental questionnaires can help to streamline the selection process by obtaining answers without having to bring the candidate in for the same information.

Telephone Interview

Another common technique is the use of the telephone interview. These interviews should only include a handful of questions and should not last longer than about 5 to 10 min. While you may obtain additional information through the telephone interview, you will probably be able to know whether or not you want to continue to evaluate the candidate after only the first 5 to 10 minutes of conversation. After a brief introduction of yourself, jumping right into the interview questions can keep you on task. This will help you to evaluate their ability to communicate their answers, formulate responses, interact professionally, and much more. You may choose to allow them to ask you questions as well. This helps the candidate to engage further, help you understand the nature of their qualifications much better, and also allow you to create a sense of motivation to continue in the process for those individuals who are highly talented.

Individual Interview

The most common approach is the individual, face-to-face interview with the candidate. This is a great opportunity to get to know the person of that more closely and assess "fit". It is typically not an ideal approach in most cases to assess technical capabilities and competency.

Panel Interview

The panel interview is simply a face-to-face interview, but with several individuals on the panel. This may include two or more people. This can allow multiple perceptions through the evaluation process which may prove valuable, especially if the incumbent in this position works with individuals throughout the organization. Be sure that the interview questions are consistent as well as the evaluation criteria so that all participants are on the same page with what is expected and desired in the position.

"In Basket" Test

An in-basket test is simply a way to put the person into the position and see how they perform. In addition to an individual interview, you may place the candidate in a scenario that simulates the job. This may include providing presentations, answering phones, working on projects, or otherwise engaging in work that would actually be accomplished through the course of a normal business day. This allows the interviewers to assess how well they perform in a "live" situation. This can prove invaluable in determining their skill level in the actual performance of duties.

On-Site Assessment

Similar to an in basket test, an on-site assessment may be a more technical approach by placing the individual into the performance of the job duties which may be of a more technical nature. For example, if you want to find out if a mechanic can actually fix a car, put them under the hood. You can do this in a number of situations that allow you to see their capability in performing the technical aspects of the work.

Other Common Evaluation Tools

Other common tools are typically those to help in the screening process rather than the assessment of qualifications. Given the large number of applicants, these may be helpful to you to ensure that the right person comes to work for you.

- Drug screening: This process is typically regulated through HR in most organizations. Keep in mind that if your organization has an established drug screening policy that is applicable to all candidates, then it must be maintained. There should be no selective utilization of the screening process – it's all or nothing.

- Criminal background check: The use of criminal background checks is very common to ensure that your work environment remains safe and protected. As you review background checks, which again may be regulated through HR, you must ensure that you do not simply base a person's qualifications on whether or not they have ever had an infraction. Some infractions, even felony cases, may not be relevant to the current position for which you are hiring. A person that may have been jailed as a minor, having been tried as an adult, 30 years ago for something that does not pertain to the job is probably not a valid reason to exclude him/her from consideration.

- Employment screening: Most references that are included on the resume and application materials tend to be those individuals who would be friendly or provide a positive recommendation about the candidate. If you believe that the individuals listed in their roles are indicative of past performance, and you're comfortable with responses, it is probably satisfactory. In other cases, you may need to ask for additional references beyond those that are included in the resume such as past supervisors, past coworkers, etc. to fully gain some insight as to their interaction and performance at other locations. Some organizations have a strict mandate to only allow information to come from HR, and that information is typically limited to specific employment information. However, if it is available and out there, you can seek after it.

- Credit information: While most background screening companies include credit checks, employers are strongly encouraged to only use that information when it is relevant or pertinent to the position. When hiring a frontline employee working in customer service, a record of a past bankruptcy five years ago may not be relevant at all to their employment. Some employers go so far as to say that if an employee does not have clean credit then they do not demonstrate integrity. When considering the impacts of the past recessions, market cycles, personal health considerations, and several other factors, an individual's credit rating may have been negatively impacted by things that may have largely been out of their control. Relevancy to the job is important, so if a person's credit history does not directly relate to his/her duties, employers are advised against using such information for employment decisions.

Conducting the Interview

Many training programs focus and the intricacies and details associated with conducting the actual interview itself. This in itself can take volumes to review the many facets of conducting the interview. As you go through the previous steps outlined in this paper, you will formulate the different pieces, processes, and activities associated with your selection process for the position. The following section provides recommendations pertaining to conducting the interview rather than the specific content of the interview.

Remember the Purpose of the Interview

The interview has two primary objectives: it is an opportunity for (1) you to get to know the candidate and assess his/her qualifications and (2) for the candidate to become familiar with you as the employer and determine whether or not to continue to pursue employment with you. Spending the entire time asking questions and getting answers may satisfy your requirements, but does not allow the candidate sufficient time in most cases to find out enough information to make his/her decision. At the same time, spending inordinate amounts of time trying to sell your organization to the candidate may send a message of desperation and at the same time not allow you to learn about the candidate. Finally, allowing the applicants to hijack the interview may provide him/her with the ability to learn more about you, but you will walk out of the interview without answers to your questions.

Staying on Track

In most interview situations, there is a schedule to follow in order to manage multiple candidates through the process. It is important that you maintain your timeframe and allow us a few variations as possible from the timeframe. You can always end an interview early, especially if it is obvious and apparent that this is not somebody who you want to continue with. It is just important that you do not go over the timeframe allotted so that you can maintain the appropriate management of your candidates. If you would truly like to learn more information about the candidate, and you are interested in continuing with them through the process, you may want to schedule another time to carry on your discussion.

Managing the Candidate's Responses

There are applicants who may hijack the interview. This may be done in several ways such as providing excessively long responses, creating questions at inappropriate times, answering questions and then getting the interviewers off track, or otherwise spending inordinate amounts of time on things other than what you need to find out in an interview process. In other situations, the individual may surprise you with a response that has the potential to create liability if handled the wrong way. For example, when asked why he wanted to join the organization for which he was interviewing, one candidate responded that it was his intention to come on board and organize a union. Without handling that situation by interjecting a response that told him that the company would respect his rights under the National Labor Relations Act, their reaction could have led to unintended liability.

As an interviewer, it is important to stay on track. If a candidate continues to speak beyond the scope of the answer, you can simply raise your hand while at the same time saying, "My apologies, but I believe that you answered what we needed and we need to continue so that we have enough time to run through the rest of the questions." Interrupting with tact and diplomacy will allow you to keep everybody on track without offending.

Knowing When to Say "When"

You will know in most cases if you want to continue to evaluate or consider hiring the person within the first 3 to 5 minutes of your interview with him or her. In some cases, it may go longer than that, but in most situations you will know whether or not you want to continue to evaluate the candidate after the first few minutes. The last thing that you want to do is to create a structure that guarantees a candidate additional steps or time in the selection process when it makes no sense to continue to do so.

As you identify your selection criteria, once you have established that the candidate is not a viable option, it may be time to let them go out of the process. This saves both you and the candidate time in pursuing something that is not going to materialize. In those situations, you may want to create certain points in the interview process where you can gain feedback, verbal or visual through body language, from other members of the interview panel to determine whether or not you should pursue the rest of the process. It does not make sense if after the first three questions you have all determined that the person is not a viable candidate to continue through the rest of the questions. You may consider some different approaches that may work for you to be able to save yourselves time and get out of interview situations when you have found that the individual in the room with you no longer proves to be a viable candidate.

Legal Considerations in Hiring

As with the actual interviewing process, an entire course could be dedicated simply to elements of employment law, litigation, and risk reduction in the hiring process. Instead, we're going to focus on some of the big-ticket items that have perhaps of the largest impacts in the hiring process. The following discussion points are not meant to be all-inclusive, but simply provide some important elements to consider through the hiring process.

Question Review

In all cases, it is important to have your interview questions and your selection processes reviewed by Human Resources to ensure legal compliance. Even if you have used the same questions in the past, you will want to ensure that they are reviewed by Human Resources prior to every interview. With how quickly laws change that pertain to employment, what may have been okay before may no longer be appropriate now.

Americans with Disabilities Act (ADA)

The Americans with Disabilities Act is focused on protecting those individuals with disabilities. While we may presume that we understand what constitutes a disability, the list grows from year-to-year as to what is protected by the law. For this reason, it is essential that if you have any questions or concerns whatsoever during the process, be sure to contact Human Resources for additional information and guidance.

Some of the most common ways in which interviewers violate the ADA include asking about an apparent disability. For example, while a job candidate may appear to be missing an arm, it is inappropriate to ask the question, "What happened to your arm?" In situations where a candidate is in a wheelchair, questions pertaining to any accident, injury, or any relationship to being in a wheelchair may be considered prejudicial. A person walking into a room with a significant limp may or may not suffer from a disability. It may be a temporary injury or it may be permanent in nature. If the limp has nothing to do with the performance of the essential functions of the job, managers must ensure that they do not question the candidate about it.

While Human Resources typically includes legal caveats in the application materials for candidates, it is important to recognize that if the candidate requests any kind of accommodation for his/her interview, that you run it past Human Resources prior to communicating a response to the candidate.

Remember that the ADA protects individuals based upon: (1) having a disability, (2) having a history of a disability, and/or (3) being perceived as having a disability. This means that the individual may not even be disabled, but if we perceive them to have a disability and treat them as such, they would then fall under the protection of the ADA. Any comments, even in joking, that may give the candidate the impression that the employer perceives him/her to have a disability, and especially if the candidate perceives that the interviewer may take their actual or potential disability status into consideration for the job, liability is created.

Ability to Perform the Essential Functions

Related to the ADA is the evaluation of the individual candidate's ability to perform the essential functions of the job. The ADA requires that the candidate be able to perform the essential functions of the job, either WITH or WITHOUT reasonable accommodation by the employer. What this means is that if a function is deemed to be essential to the job, and they are physically unable to perform even a single function, the employer does not need to accommodate that employee. They are not qualified to perform the job if they cannot meet the requirements of ALL essential functions EITHER with or without reasonable accommodation. It is ultimately up to the employer to decide whether or not they will accommodate performance of an ESSENTIAL function.

Some employers are more relaxed in their willingness to accommodate situations where the individual cannot perform one or more essential functions without accommodation by the employer. Other employers are very strict in ensuring that each employee is able to perform ALL essential functions without reasonable accommodation. It is important for you to check with Human Resources to determine the flexibility that you have provided reasonable accommodation in some cases. Whenever a situation arises where it appears that the candidate is unable to perform the essential functions unless they have some kind of accommodation, you should contact Human Resources immediately to assist you.

Stay Focused on the Job

All questions, assessments, practices, forms, etc. related to the selection process MUST have relevance to the position itself for which the candidate has applied. It is not uncommon to hear supervisors ask questions at the beginning of an interview about whether the candidate has family, kids, spouse, etc. However, all of these (family status, marital status) are protected by state and federal law. Staying on track and sticking to questions that are cordial, professional, and job-related can still help to build a relationship with the candidate without having to pursue questions in areas that are off-limits.

First Impressions

First impressions are important when it comes to professionalism in the workplace. Many things are communicated, both verbally and visually, by an individual through his/her demeanor, appearance, and behavior. One area where managers get into legal trouble is the inappropriate evaluation of first impressions. If the first impressions are relevant to the performance of the position, then those are impressions that can be used and taken into consideration when evaluating the candidate. Other impressions, however, if they are not related to the position itself, should not be considered as part of the evaluation criteria.

One of the most common areas of trouble is when managers want to hire people who are just like them. This often translates into the same gender, race, nationality, age, etc. While a manager may not do this consciously, they may inadvertently do it unless they focus on the position itself and how the first impressions relate to the performance and execution of the position. Without this consideration, managers will often perpetuate themselves in their employees. This will also leads to departments that are all of the same gender, the same nationality, the same backgrounds, the same experiences, etc. While this is not necessarily illegal, it does limit your ability to expand your horizons and bring in a diverse perspective which may ultimately hurt your ability to remain competitive in the marketplace.

"Fit"

Managers will often talk about how an employee "fits" in a position, in a department, and in an organization. This typically relates to the nature of the individual and how he/she will fit in to the culture of the workgroup or organization. These measures of "fit" are typically based upon perceptions, communication skills, personality, attitudes, and other verbal and nonverbal cues that tell the manager whether or not they would be easy to assimilate into the work environment.

Fit is important. Fit is one of the most significant intangibles that has the greatest impact to the actual demonstrable performance of the individual and/or the department. If an employee cannot get along with others or does not work well with others, this will not only affect his/her performance, but also will impact the performance of others with whom he or she works.

As you assess fit, keep in mind that it must be related to the position. This not only takes into account the job description requirements, but also the nature of the position, the culture of the organization, the other personalities with him he/she will be working, your management style, etc. When you evaluate fit with the candidate, be sure to evaluate those measures based upon the actual position itself and avoid focusing only on others and how closely they look just like you.

Case Study: Hiring a Technical Position

A position opened up in your department for a technical machinist. You have the standard questions based on the job description and your Top Performer Profile of what an ideal candidate looks like.

You want to find out more about a particular candidate's backgrounds and abilities, but more specifically how competent he/she is in performing technical functions that require knowledge of technical duties (e.g., ability to build working models, operate machines to very technical specifications, assess and modify machinery according to specifications, etc.).

Traditionally, your primary approach to hiring a candidate has been through the sit-down interview. To find out this additional information, you may consider specific questions asked during the interview that could enlighten you on their background and capabilities. From your past experience you have noticed that many people who are successful in this role typically have outside interests, hobbies, and projects that include the use of their hands in technical or complex activities (e.g., model building, woodworking, auto mechanics).

One question that you have asked in the past is:

"What are some of your hobbies, interests, and activities outside of work?"

From your perspective, you may be looking for answers that indicate some of the "sweet spot" answers such as model building, woodworking, and auto mechanics. So what can go wrong with asking a question such as this?

A question such as this, without additional refinement or context, could open up the door to a number of unintended consequences. Open-ended questions such as this could result in responses such as...

- References to their kids and family (pregnancy, family and marital status are protected in the state of Washington)
- Participation in nonprofit organizations that may appear controversial and that engage in protected activities (e.g. participation with the local AIDS foundation, political action groups, or even Boy Scouts)
- Taking care of elderly parents (which may lead to questions that would apply to FMLA protected leave)
- Engaging in activities related to a local union (with such activities being protected under the National Labor Relations Act)
- Attending courses and programs relating to personal concerns (such as physical therapy, Alcoholics Anonymous, or other protected activities and associations)

You may think that this is far-fetched and unreasonable, and that it would never happen with your applicants. Such an innocent question would never result in those kinds of responses, right?

No matter how hard we work at it, there will always be some level of subjectivity to the hiring process and there'll always be a certain level of exposure to risk involved when we interview candidates. The key is not to eliminate any and all risk, but to reduce that where possible. While the intention of the question makes sense, and your past experience may have proven this to be somewhat effective in past candidates sharing interests that led to a decision on your part, questions such as this may unintentionally open yourself to greater liability and risk.

In situations such as this, we may believe that we are unable to ask this question and therefore are unable to find out the information for which we are searching. Instead, let's take a different approach to determine other ways to uncover the information you are looking for.

Let's begin by determining what we are looking for. While the specific requirements will vary depending upon the position, let's consider the following six areas of priority:

- Technical skills related to the specific requirements needed as a technical machinist
- Technical competence to be able to adapt to specific machinery and jobs
- Technical capabilities such as independent critical thinking and problem solving skills
- Technical proficiency to understand and interpret specific designs
- Ability to apply technical concepts to design, build, and modify parts and equipment
- Ability to design, interpret designs for, and build products and equipment

So how do you find out if a person has these to the desired level for which you're looking?

One step is to consider the best way to determine the level proficiency and skill in each of these areas. Considering the types of selection processes at our disposal, perhaps we can consider which approach(es) would be more effective in this evaluation.

- Sit-down Interview: In a situation where we want to evaluate a candidate's technical skills, the sit-down interview has certain strengths and weaknesses. Strengths can be identified through the development of questions that allow for the candidate to describe his/her functional literacy related to the topic. As you ask a question specific to the candidate's capabilities, you may be able to assess their level of knowledge, familiarity, and even some proficiency based upon the vocabulary, language, and idioms used in the response. The weakness to using the interview to assess level of proficiency is that the candidate can talk a good talk, and convince you that he/she knows what they're talking about. Yet without putting them in the situation to clearly demonstrate their proficiency, they are still only talking about it. A sit-down interview process may not be the most effective way to evaluate levels of proficiency.

- Hands-on test: In some situations, it would make sense to create a hands-on testing approach to determine the level of skill and proficiency by the candidate. If the desired outcome is to assess the candidate's ability to operate the specific machine that is used in your workplace, and the candidate clearly indicates that he/she is familiar with and proficient at using that equipment, you may have the candidate walk through an overview and explanation of how to work and operate the machinery. (You may be a little guarded in letting them actually operate the machine as they are a candidate and not an employee, which may create potential for greater liability.)

  In other situations, you may have a set of design specifications for them to evaluate and explain or interpret for you. You may also have a model that is available for them to build, craft, adapt, etc. as you see fit which would demonstrate their abilities. Still another situations, you may describe the outcomes and is desired and provide them with a box of materials with which to craft the solution.

Rather than focusing entirely upon the specific question that you want to ask, you can instead focus on the information that you want to know and then formulate your processes around finding out information from the candidate about their level of knowledge, skills, proficiency, or capacity in those areas. Not only does this help to reduce the potential for liability, but it typically also improves the ability for you as the interviewer to clearly evaluate the level of proficiency and performance by the candidate.

Evaluating the Results

The final point of this discussion is the evaluation of the results. After the selection process is completed, and all steps have been reviewed, it is time to evaluate the results of the performance of your candidates. Throughout the process, you probably were able to effectively eliminate candidates as you moved from step to step. Having created your Top Performer Profile, this should have created an overview of the criteria for which you are looking in a candidate. It should also have helped you to be confident in letting candidates go when it was established that they did not qualify for the position.

When you get to the end of the evaluation process, or even one of the steps of the evaluation process, it is time to compare what you were looking for and the outcomes of the interview or selection processes. Consider the following as you evaluate results.

Did You Get Enough Information to Make a Decision?

As you progress through the process, you may recognize a few things along the way. For example, what you were looking for as outlined in your Top Performer Profile may have been modified as you continued to visit with candidates. For example, some candidates may have brought out new talents or ideas that you had not considered before. If this is the case, there is not a reason why you cannot incorporate that into your evaluation criteria as you go – so long as you are consistent. This flexibility allows you to reduce the rigidity which may expand the opportunities to find an ideal candidate.

As you finalize the process, be sure to consider whether or not you obtained enough information to make an informed decision. Keep in mind that there is no way to have 100% of all the information to make a decision. That will never happen. Even when they come on board, how they perform the first month may differ in the second month and throughout their employment. The key is to ensure that you have ENOUGH information upon which to base your decision. If you did not, do not be afraid to take one more step to evaluate the candidate so that you can obtain enough information to move forward. Just be sure to avoid paralysis by analysis by trying to collect more information than is reasonable through the selection process prior to making a decision.

Candidate Performance

As you near the end of the selection process, you may be satisfied or perhaps disappointed with the results. In cases of disappointment, and especially in cases where there appear not to be any qualified applicants, you may want to take a step back and reconsider your evaluation criteria. Now that it is complete, did you have the right list of requirements? Were your thresholds too tight? Were your evaluation criteria inconsistent or measurements too subjective?

It is not uncommon for a hiring manager to get to the end and not find what he/she was looking for, only to find out that they may have been looking for something more than was reasonable given the job classification, the compensation offered, or other terms and conditions related to the position. If that be the case, you may want to go back and reconsider some of your evaluation criteria, make some adjustments, and then reevaluate the outcomes of the candidates' performance prior to making any final decisions.

"Selection" versus "Settling"

Remember that this is a SELECTION process. This means that you are out to select the best candidate with the best talent available to you to meet your needs. As you go to the grocery store shopping for produce, you typically go through a selection process to find the best produce. It is generally not going to be the produce that is right in front of you. It takes some evaluation and review to find the right produce that meets your needs. At the same time, if you cannot find produce that meets your needs at this particular grocery store, do you just settle for produce that is just *not as bad* as the rest? In most cases, if quality matters, you are going to go to a different grocery store and begin the selection process again.

The same applies when evaluating candidates for a position. If you do not find what you're looking for, and nothing that is available to you during the selection process will meet your needs, it may be time to start again. By settling for the "best of the worst", or the candidates who are just "not as bad" as the rest, chances are good that you're making the wrong hire. The consequences of making a bad hiring decision are very costly.

While it does take additional time and it does cost additional productivity by starting all over, in the end you will find that taking that approach will cost you far less when you find the right candidate than to hire the wrong candidate. Hiring the wrong person can result in poor productivity, poor morale throughout the department, increase liability, and a long list of negative impacts. It may take an extra month or so to find a candidate through new process, yet in the end you save considerable time by not having to replace the poor performer and fix the mistakes that were caused by him/her.

Conclusion

The discussion in this white paper was not meant to be all-inclusive or exhaustive in nature. Instead, it was intended to provide an overview and a recap of some of the primary considerations to take into account as you engage in the hiring process.

There are volumes of books and other information out there to help improve each aspect of the hiring process. While it is not critical to spend inordinate amounts of time finding those materials, you're encouraged to continue your learning to improve your skill at hiring the best talent.

The talent you hire can make or break your company. You can be the talent that you need to gain that extra competitiveness, or it could be the poor talent that can drive you into failure. Take the time to know what you want and develop your selection processes around that. As you do, not only will you find the process to run smoother and more efficiently, but the outcome of hiring top talent will improve as well.

www.ingramcontent.com/pod-product-compliance
Lightning Source LLC
Chambersburg PA
CBHW050426180526
45159CB00005B/2425